LISTEN TO YOUR HEART

LISTEN TO
YOUR HEART

Kenneth W. Hagin

Unless otherwise indicated, all Scripture quotations are taken from the King James Version of the Bible.

19 18 17 16 15 14 13   14 13 12 11 10 09 08

Listen to Your Heart
ISBN–13: 978-0-89276-726-7
ISBN–10: 0-89276-726-X

In the U.S. write:
Kenneth Hagin Ministries
P.O. Box 50126
Tulsa, OK 74150-0126
1-888-28-FAITH
www.rhema.org

In Canada write:
Kenneth Hagin Ministries of Canada
P.O. Box 335, Station D
Etobicoke (Toronto), Ontario
Canada M9A 4X3
1-866-70-RHEMA
www.rhemacanada.org

Contents

Contents

Acknowledgment

In writing a book about the subject of being led by the Holy Spirit, I want to acknowledge the great influence my dad, Rev. Kenneth E. Hagin, had on my life. As far back as I can remember, Dad always endeavored to live his life according to the Word of God and to be led by the Holy Spirit in every situation.

Dad's teaching on this subject, including his book *How You Can Be Led by the Spirit of God,* and his own example as he lived a Spirit-led life, helped me learn early in life how to obey the Holy Spirit's leading as I've listened to my heart.

Chapter 1
What Is the Heart?

The SPIRIT OF MAN is the candle of the Lord, searching all the inward parts of the belly.

—Proverbs 20:27

Just because you're a Christian doesn't necessarily mean you will be successful in fulfilling God's plan for your life. Certainly, if you've accepted Jesus Christ as Savior and Lord of your life, you will go to Heaven one day. But it's quite possible for you to live your entire life here on the earth and miss out on fulfilling your destiny and receiving the rich blessings your Heavenly Father has planned for you.

The only way you can successfully run the race God has set before you (Heb. 12:1) and live in His abundant provision is by learning how to receive guidance from the Holy Spirit as you *listen to your heart*—your recreated human spirit. Learning to be led by the Holy Spirit according to the Word of God is the most important lesson you'll ever learn in life. This book is intended to give you practical insight to help you learn how to listen to your heart.

What am I referring to when I say "listen to your *heart*"? Are you supposed to listen to your physical heart—to the muscle that pumps blood throughout your body? Of course not. Then what "heart" are you supposed to listen to? You can't learn to listen to your heart if you aren't sure scripturally what the heart *is*.

1

Even in the world when people use the term, "heart," they are usually not referring to the literal, physical heart. For instance, people sometimes say, "I mean it from the bottom of my heart." Or a person might be described as having "a big heart." People understand these phrases don't refer to the physical organ inside the body that pumps blood. Even in the world, most people know there is more to man than the physical body.

Of course, man does possess a physical organ called a heart. But the Bible teaches us that man possesses a *spiritual* heart as well. In fact, there are 830 references in the Bible to man's heart, and very few of them refer to the physical organ that pumps blood throughout the body. Most of the scriptural references to the heart refer to the unseen center of man's being—the inward man (2 Cor. 4:16; 1 Peter 3:4).

Many times in the Old Testament the word "heart" refers to this intangible center of man's being. For instance, in First Chronicles, David speaks of being knit together in his heart with others.

1 CHRONICLES 12:16–17
16 And there came of the children of Benjamin and Judah to the hold unto David.
17 And David went out to meet them, and answered and said unto them, If ye be come peaceably unto me to help me, MINE HEART SHALL BE KNIT UNTO YOU: but if ye be come to betray me to mine enemies, seeing there is no wrong in mine hands, the God of our fathers look thereon, and rebuke it.

David certainly wasn't talking here about knitting his *physical* heart with the Israelites! Likewise, when the Bible says in First Chronicles 12:38 that the people of Israel were of *one heart* to make David king, it is talk-ing about the Israelites' unified *desire* and *will* to make

David king. It had nothing to do with the people's physical hearts. A literal interpretation of these references to the heart would be ridiculous, wouldn't it? Yet if you follow some people's teaching about the heart to its logical conclusion, that's the way you would have to interpret those verses. Some people do not recognize the existence of man's spiritual heart, and they try to explain the nature of man's being only in physical terms. But the *nature* or essence of man is spiritual, not physical. In fact man *is* a spirit; he *possesses* a soul; and he *lives* in a body (*see* Gen. 1:26–27; John 4:24; 1 Thess. 5:23; Heb. 4:12).

In the New Testament, the Bible further explains what the heart is. Let's look at a few verses that help answer the question, "What is the heart of man?"

MARK 11:23
23 For verily I say unto you, That whosoever shall say unto this mountain, Be thou removed, and be thou cast into the sea; and shall not doubt in his HEART, but shall believe that those things which he saith shall come to pass; he shall have whatsoever he saith.

ROMANS 10:8–10
8 But what saith it? The word is nigh thee, even in thy mouth, and in thy HEART: that is, the word of faith, which we preach;
9 That if thou shalt confess with thy mouth the Lord Jesus, and shalt believe in thine HEART that God hath raised him from the dead, thou shalt be saved.
10 For with the HEART man believeth unto righteousness; and with the mouth confession is made unto salvation.

Of course, these verses are talking about something other than the physical organ in your chest called the heart. These verses say it's with man's *spiritual* heart

that he doubts or believes. The heart muscle itself has no
ability to doubt or to believe, or to express anything for
that matter. It has no ability to do anything except con-
tract and expand and pump blood throughout the body.
No, when the Bible refers to believing with the *heart*, it is
referring to something entirely different than a physical
organ—it's referring to man's *spiritual* heart or inward
nature.

Man's spiritual heart is also called "the hidden man of
the heart."

1 PETER 3:4
**4   But let it be THE HIDDEN MAN OF THE HEART, in
that which is not corruptible, even the ornament of a
meek and quiet spirit, which is in the sight of God of
great price.**

What does this verse mean by "the hidden man of the
heart"? It is referring to the same thing Paul is talking about in Second Corinthians 4:16 when he says,
". . . *though our outward man perish, yet THE INWARD
MAN is renewed day by day."*

We see from these scriptures that the heart of man is
much more than a physical organ. The physical heart is
just a part of the outward man—the physical man—which
will one day perish. But the hidden man of the heart or
the inward man is the *real* man—the spirit man who will
live forever.

Therefore, in order to learn how to listen to your heart
or your spirit, you must be aware of the fact that you *are*
a spirit being. If you live only conscious of your physical
body and your feelings, you will never learn to be led by
the Holy Spirit through your own spirit (Rom. 8:14).

The Bible says that God communicates with His children
through their heart or spirit—the *real* man.

ROMANS 8:16
16 The Spirit itself [himself] **beareth witness WITH OUR SPIRIT, that we are the children of God.**

The Holy Spirit bears witness with our *spirit* that we are the children of God. That means God communicates with us through our spirits because God is a Spirit (John 4:24), and He made us in His image as spirit beings (Gen. 1:26; 2 Cor. 5:17). Because our *spirits* are born again under the New Covenant, we can't commune with God in *soul* or in *body*, but only in *spirit*—with our recreated spirits.

When we are born again and our spirits are made alive unto God, God communes with us through the spirit man on the inside or the hidden man of the heart. Proverbs 20:27 says, *"The SPIRIT of man is the CANDLE of the Lord, searching all the inward parts of the belly."* Notice the *spirit* of man, not the *body* or *soul* of man, is the candle of the Lord.

In modern-day terms, we could say the spirit of man is the *light bulb* of the Lord. What does a light bulb do? It gives illumination. When a light bulb is turned on, darkness is dispelled.

In the same way, when your spirit becomes a new creature in Christ (2 Cor. 5:17) and is made alive unto God, then the light of the Lord, the Holy Spirit, comes to abide within you to give you illumination (John 14:17, 23). When the Holy Spirit dwells within you, communication with the Lord through your spirit is then possible.

Therefore, you can be led by the Holy Spirit in every situation of life as you learn how to listen to your heart or spirit, which is the candle or "the light bulb" of the Lord (Prov. 20:27). And the leading of the Holy Spirit through your heart brings light and understanding and dispels darkness. This is the way you are to be led and receive direction from God.

If you want to successfully follow God's plan and purpose for your life, you need to live constantly aware that you are a spirit being. In other words, in every situation in life you must learn to respond from your *heart* or spirit, not from your *head* or from your five *physical senses*. Your mind and your body have not been born again or recreated. Therefore, if you allow yourself to be led by your mind and your body, you'll be living according to natural circumstances instead of by the supernatural power of God's Word.

So when you seek direction from God, don't try to figure out God's plan for you with your mental faculties or your physical senses. It's easy to try to do that. Your mind can begin to think, *Let's see: This happened and that happened. Therefore, I should do this.* However, when you draw a conclusion from your own mental reasoning, that conclusion can seem right at first, but it can end in failure if it's not God's plan for your life.

The Bible says you are to walk by *faith* in God and not by *sight* (2 Cor. 5:7). So if you are to live according to your spirit, you must not necessarily be moved by what your physical senses tell you about a situation or circumstance. Rather, you need to be moved by what God's Word and the Holy Spirit tell you.

Of course, it's true that at times your physical senses give you information you should heed. For instance, when you touch a hot stove, your sense of touch tells you, "Take your hand off that stove *quickly!*" And you need to obey that! But I'm talking about those situations or problems you face in life for which there is no solution in the natural or in the physical realm. Your physical senses might tell you, "Run from this problem!" and your mind might tell you, "There's no way out!"

But in that kind of situation, you need to receive the Holy Spirit's direction and stand on God's Word without wavering. You need to make the decision to believe God's Word no matter what you see, feel, or think.

Successfully following God's plan for your life depends on what you choose to listen to—your physical senses or the Word of God and the leading of the Holy Spirit. In spiritual matters, if you just listen to your physical senses or your mind, you are in danger of losing your joy and the victories God intends you to have in life according to His Word.

For example, if you focus your attention on what you hear on the news, you can become depressed thinking about the problems in this world today. You can begin wondering, *How are we ever going to make it?*

But it doesn't matter what your mind or your physical senses tell you! It doesn't matter what the newscaster says! Regardless of what circumstances look like, the Word of God is still true. And if you get quiet on the inside and begin listening to what your heart or spirit is saying, the Holy Spirit will minister the truth of God's Word to you.

If you are a Christian, your God is the King of kings and the Lord of lords. He can take care of you! Remember in the Old Testament, it is recorded that God took care of the children of Israel, even in the wilderness. For forty years He protected His people and led them by a pillar of cloud by day and a pillar of fire by night (Exod. 13:21). He fed them heavenly manna and kept their shoes and clothing from wearing out (Deut. 8:3–4).

God has promised to take care of *you* too! Your answer may not come the way you have it figured out in your mind. But if you will only trust God and learn to listen to the Holy Spirit's direction to your heart, God will see you through to victory in every situation!

Chapter 2

Dividing the Soul
and the Spirit

*For the WORD OF GOD is quick, and powerful, and
sharper than any twoedged sword, piercing even to the
DIVIDING ASUNDER OF SOUL AND SPIRIT, and of
the joints and marrow, and is a discerner of the thoughts
and intents of the heart.*

—Hebrews 4:12

We saw that the heart is the spirit or the inward man
and that God communicates with us through our spirit
(Prov. 20:27; Rom. 8:14, 16). We *are* spirit beings. But the
Bible also teaches that we each *possess* a soul and we *live
in* a body (1 Thess. 5:23).

With the body we contact the *physical* realm. With our
spirit or heart we contact the *spiritual* realm. So what
realm do we contact with the soul? The soul includes the
mind, will, and emotions. Therefore, with the soul we contact the *intellectual* and *emotional* realms.

It's easy to define what our body is, because it's the
part of us that's visible and that contacts the tangible,
physical realm. Through the five physical senses of sight,
hearing, touch, taste, and smell, the body provides us
with the information we need to discern the natural world
we live in. So we can easily distinguish between our outward man, the physical body, and our inward man, the
spirit or heart.

9

It's much more difficult to distinguish between our soul and our spirit, because they are the intangible, unseen parts of our nature. Yet it is vitally important to learn how to correctly distinguish between the soul and the spirit. Without understanding the difference between the soul and spirit, we would not be able to successfully learn how to listen to our heart and be led by the Holy Spirit instead of by our soul in the situations of life.

Controversy has raged for many years over this issue of distinguishing between the soul and spirit. Many theologians believe that the soul and the spirit are the same thing. However, the Bible makes a definite distinction between the two.

For instance, Paul differentiates between the spirit, soul, and body of man in his prayer to the Thessalonian Church: "*. . . I pray God your whole SPIRIT and SOUL and BODY be preserved blameless unto the coming of our Lord Jesus Christ*" (1 Thess. 5:23). And Hebrews 4:12 shows us that the soul and spirit can be *separated* by God's Word. Therefore, the soul and spirit must be two separate entities.

HEBREWS 4:12
12 For the word of God is quick, and powerful, and sharper than any twoedged sword, piercing even to the DIVIDING ASUNDER of SOUL and SPIRIT, and of the joints and marrow [body], and is a discerner of the thoughts and intents of the heart.

The Word of God divides asunder or separates the soul and spirit of man because they are two different entities. There would be no need to divide them if they were the same. For instance, if you try to separate water from water, you will find it is impossible. You cannot separate something from itself. A container of water divided into two parts still equals *water*.

But two distinct entities *can* be separated from each other. For example, when dirt and water are mixed together in a container, the muddy water is still basically made up of two different elements: dirt and water. If the water isn't disturbed for a period of time, the mud settles to the bottom of the container. In other words, the mud can be separated from the water, because dirt and water are distinct entities.

In a similar sense, even though the soul and spirit are intertwined within the nature of each person, they can be separated from each other because they are two separate entities. But they can *only* be separated by the Word of God. We need to understand what the Word says about the soul and the spirit of man to know how to distinguish between them.

In First Corinthians, Paul distinguishes between the *spirit* and the *mind*, which is part of the soul of man.

1 CORINTHIANS 14:14–15
14 For if I pray in an unknown tongue, my SPIRIT pray-eth, but my UNDERSTANDING [mind] is unfruitful.
15 What is it then? I will pray with the SPIRIT, and I will pray with the UNDERSTANDING [mind] also: I will sing with the SPIRIT, and I will sing with the UNDERSTANDING [mind] also.

In this passage, Paul says that when you pray in tongues, you are praying with your *spirit*. Your natural understanding or mind is often unfruitful or *unproductive* (1 Cor. 14:14 *Amp.*). In other words, your *mind* doesn't necessarily always know what you are saying. That's because you don't pray in an unknown tongue out of your mind. When you pray in tongues, you are speaking secret truths to God with your *spirit* (1 Cor. 14:2 *Amp.*).

The Bible also says you are building yourself up when you pray in other tongues: *"But ye, beloved, BUILDING UP YOURSELVES on your most holy faith, PRAYING IN THE HOLY GHOST"* (Jude 20).

What does that verse mean by "building *yourselves* up"? What part of your nature do you build up by praying in other tongues? You certainly aren't building up your *body*! If you want to build up your body, you could lift weights at the local gym.

So we know that praying in other tongues doesn't build up your body. And praying in other tongues doesn't build up your *soul* either. You can build up or train your mind, which is a part of your soul, through intellectual study. Or you can also *renew* your mind with the Word of God (Rom. 12:2) so you can learn to walk according to the Word. But when you "build yourself up on your most holy faith" by praying in other tongues, you are building up your *spirit* or *heart*—the *real* man on the inside (1 Cor. 14:4, 14).

So you pray in tongues with your spirit, not with your mind or your soul. You also *worship* God with your spirit because God is a Spirit. Of course, your body and soul can become involved in worship. But under the New Covenant, we worship God with our recreated spirit—in spirit and in truth—because we've been born again (John 4:24).

As we worship God with our spirit, the power of God's Presence sometimes affects our emotions and body too. For instance, people sometimes say, "Oh, I feel so good when I worship the Lord." People can get so full of the Holy Spirit in their spirit that His power also spills over into the physical and emotional realm.

What else does the Bible say about the difference between the soul and the spirit? We know that when a person is born again, his *spirit* becomes new, not his mind or body.

2 CORINTHIANS 5:17
17 Therefore if any man be in Christ, he is a NEW CREATURE [in his spirit]: **old things are passed away; behold, all things are become new.**

What part of you became a new creature in Christ when you were born again? Did your body suddenly change at the moment of your salvation? Of course not. And your soulish thoughts and emotions didn't change overnight either, did they? If your soul became brand-new in the new birth, Paul wouldn't have told believers they still have to renew their minds with the Word of God (Rom. 12:2).

No, it was your *spirit* that became a new creation in Christ the moment you were born again. Old things passed away and all things became new in your *inward* man, the hidden man of the heart (1 Peter 3:4).

The outward man still wanted to do the same things it did *before* salvation. That's why the Bible tells believers to present their bodies as a living sacrifice to God and to keep their bodies under the dominion or control of their spirits (Rom. 12:1; 1 Cor. 9:27). We'll talk later about what believers are to do with their outward man—the body or the flesh.

Also, a person's mind still wants to think the same thoughts it did before he was born again. Baby Christians often get confused over this because they don't know how to rightly divide or distinguish between their soul and their spirit. They think their soul and spirit are the same. For example, if they think wrong thoughts, they might say, "I don't understand it! I thought I was born again. But if I'm saved, why in the world am I still thinking these terrible thoughts?"

But the soul isn't born again at the moment of salvation. Only the spirit is recreated and made alive unto God. Only in the spirit of man do old things pass away and all things become new.

> **EZEKIEL 36:26**
> 26 A NEW HEART also will I give you, and a NEW SPIRIT will I put within you: and I will take away the stony heart. . . .

God has recreated your spirit. Now the Bible says there is something *you* must do about the saving of your *soul*. How do you get your soul saved? Only by receiving the engrafted Word into your heart and mind.

> **JAMES 1:21**
> 21 Wherefore lay apart all filthiness and superfluity of naughtiness, and RECEIVE with meekness THE ENGRAFTED WORD, which is able to SAVE YOUR SOULS.

This verse says you are to lay aside all filthiness and "superfluity of naughtiness" in your life. *The American Standard Version* puts it this way: "putting away all filthiness and *overflowing of wickedness*." The way you are able to put away sin is by receiving the Word of God into your heart and mind so that the Word can "save your soul."

What does the Bible mean by the phrase, "save your soul"? Psalm 23:3 gives us the same idea when it says, *"He* [the Lord] *RESTORETH my soul. . . ."* And then in the Book of Romans, the Bible talks about *renewing the mind*, which is a part of the soul.

ROMANS 12:2
2 And be not conformed to this world: but BE YE
TRANSFORMED BY THE RENEWING OF YOUR
MIND, that ye may prove what is that good, and
acceptable, and perfect, will of God.

The words "restore" and "renew" both mean *to make
extensive changes in* or *to make like new*. For instance,
an antique chair might still be a good piece of furniture
even though the wood is scratched and the chair doesn't
look new anymore. And if you owned an old chair, you
wouldn't necessarily have to go out and buy a new one.
With a little skill and the right tools, you could *restore* it
and make it look like new again.

Your spirit isn't renewed or restored like an old piece
of furniture is restored. No, your spirit was *recreated* in
the new birth. You became a new creature in your spirit—
your inward man.

But as you receive the Word of God into your heart
and mind, your *mind* is renewed and you are transformed
more and more into the image of Jesus (Rom. 8:29). As
you renew your mind with the Word of God, your *soul* is
restored and you begin to think and operate in line with
the Word. That helps you keep your body and your emotions under the control of your spirit and enables you to
live right before God continually.

I knew a young man years ago whose testimony was
a striking example of the power of God's Word to renew
one's mind. Before this young man was saved, he had
almost destroyed his mind by using drugs. No one could
hold a conversation with him for more than two minutes
at a time without losing the young man's attention.

Then this young man received Jesus as his Savior.
Because he didn't have anywhere else to go, the pastor allowed him to stay at the church and work as the

janitor. He was given a Bible and a tape recorder, along with some Bible teaching tapes.

The pastor told this young man, "Whenever you can, listen to these tapes while you work. And when you aren't working, read the Bible. Read it as much as you can. If you lose your concentration, stop and do something else for a while. Then pick up your Bible again and keep on reading."

The young man did what the pastor suggested. Within two years, that man's mind was as sharp as it had ever been. In fact, four years after he was born again, he designed a sophisticated loan program to help the church building project. The banker who dealt with the church considered the loan program a masterpiece and wanted to hire the young man to work for him!

Think about it! Four years earlier, no one could hold a decent conversation with this young man because his mind had been almost completely destroyed by drugs. But then he began to study the Word until his mind became restored. And within a few years, he was well on his way to success in life. There is power in the Word of God!

The same transforming power in God's Word can work for you to renew your mind and restore your soul. But *you* are the one who has to make the decision to renew your mind with the Word of God. It is vitally important you make that decision. God wants your response to every situation in life to be from your spirit based on His Word. You can only respond that way when your mind is renewed by the Word of God.

If you are not continually renewing your mind with the Word of God, you will be more likely to respond to situations the way you used to before you were born again. But if you will continually renew your mind, you will be able to respond from your heart, your recreated spirit, and it will be much easier to resist temptation to sin. In fact, once you begin to daily renew your mind with the Word, you'll find you don't have as much trouble with temptation as you did in the past.

Many times Christians pray earnestly, "Oh, Lord, help me overcome temptation." But, actually, you overcome temptation by hiding the Word of God in your heart (Ps. 119:11) and by allowing the Word to renew your mind. When your thinking is in line with God's Word, you will be able to resist temptation and keep your thoughts and emotions in control. That is how you walk uprightly before God in your conduct.

As long as you live on this earth, the devil will never stop trying to tempt you to sin. Therefore, if you expect to be successful in your Christian walk, you can never stop renewing your mind with the Word. Renewing your mind is a continual process.

Christians stumble and get into sin when they stop renewing their mind with the Word and begin filling their mind with worldly, sinful thoughts. Believers can't fill their minds with the Word one day and fill it with ungodly thoughts the next day and expect to be successful Christians.

For instance, if you feed your mind soap operas or worldly movies, you can expect your mind to think wrong thoughts. And if you feed your mind the wrong kind of "diet" long enough, you're eventually going to begin acting on what you've been thinking.

But if you continually fill your mind with the truth of God's Word, then when the enemy tempts you, your mind will think right thoughts and your mouth will speak according to the Word you've hidden in your heart. You will be able to resist the devil's strategies and overcome the temptation to sin through the power of the Word you've sown in your heart.

I said earlier you must learn how to listen to your heart if you want to successfully follow God's plan for your life. But there is no way you can follow God's plan for your life unless you take time to renew your mind with the Word.

The truth is, you can only follow the Holy Spirit's leading in your own spirit if your mind is continually renewed with the Word of God. You become more sensitive to the things of God when your mind is renewed with the Word.

If you'll continually fill your mind with God's Word, you'll find yourself responding to circumstances in line with the Word rather than from your emotions or according to the way you used to think. So just stay faithful to daily receive the engrafted Word into your heart and mind. By doing that, your soul will continually be restored or saved (James 1:21), and it will become easier and easier for you to listen to your heart and follow the Holy Spirit's leading in your life.

Chapter 3
Keeping the Body
Under Subjection

But I KEEP UNDER MY BODY, and bring it into subjection: lest that by any means, when I have preached to others, I myself should be a castaway.

—1 Corinthians 9:27

You *are* a spirit; you *have* a soul; and you *live in* a body. Your spirit must be recreated or born again, and your soul must be renewed with the Word of God. But what about your body? What are you to do with your body —the house you live in (2 Cor. 5:1)? Remember, your body is *not* the real you; your *spirit* is the real you.

Most Christians don't live like they are spirit beings indwelt by the Spirit of the Almighty God. Many are more body-conscious than they are spirit-conscious, allowing their bodies to control the way they live. It shouldn't be that way. A Christian who lives only in the natural realm according to his physical senses will not be able to accurately listen to his heart and follow the Holy Spirit's leading.

The Bible says your spirit has a part to play in controlling your body. Notice in First Corinthians 9:27, Paul said, "... *I keep under MY BODY, and bring IT into subjection. ...*" Who is the "I" Paul is referring to? If he considered his *body* to be the real Paul, he wouldn't have said it like that. He would have said, "I keep *myself* under and bring *myself* into subjection."

19

Paul knew he was a spirit being who lived in a body. And the real Paul, his spirit man within, was to keep his body under subjection or control. Paul's inward man controlled the behavior of his outward man.

Paul made a strong statement in his letter to the Church at Rome, telling believers what to do with their bodies.

ROMANS 12:1
1 I beseech you therefore, brethren, by the mercies of God, that ye PRESENT YOUR BODIES A LIVING SACRIFICE, holy, acceptable unto God, which is your reasonable service.

Paul said, *"I BESEECH you . . . that ye present your bodies. . . ."* That word "beseech" means *to beg*. Paul considered presenting our bodies to God as a living sacrifice important enough to *beg* us to do it. He recognized that we can't live a victorious Christian life without presenting our bodies to God.

Also, you need to understand that Paul wasn't talking to sinners; he was talking to believers. He was telling people who are new creatures in Christ that *they* need to do something with their bodies.

Yes, when you are a new creature in Christ, old things have passed away and all things have become new (2 Cor. 5:17). But that is only true regarding your *inward* man. Your spirit is the new creation; your body didn't change at all when you were born again. Your body will always want to do things it is not supposed to do.

If your body never wanted to do what's wrong, there would be no reason for Paul to state, "I keep my body under" (1 Cor. 9:27). You don't have to *keep* something under control that doesn't have a tendency *to get out of control*.

For instance, as long as your car is parked, you don't have to try to control the direction it's going. But when you begin to drive the car down the road, you have to guide the car with the steering wheel or you will lose control of the vehicle, and it will probably crash into something.

In much the same way, your spirit needs to control your body. As long as you are alive on this earth, your body is going to want to do things it's not supposed to do. If you—the spirit man on the inside—don't control your body by presenting it as a living sacrifice to God, your body will begin to control you. And if you continually sow to the flesh instead of walking according to the Spirit, the Bible says you will reap corruption and cause great havoc in your life (Gal. 6:8).

That's why it is so important to keep your body under subjection to your spirit and learn how to listen to your heart. Your recreated spirit doesn't have a sin problem. Your spirit wants to obey the Word and follow the leading of the Holy Spirit. Your problems will be with your outward man or your body and your unrenewed mind because your body will always want to fulfill the desires of the flesh. Therefore, if you want to live a victorious Christian life, your *inward* man must control your *outward* man (Gal. 5:16–18).

How do you keep your body in subjection to your spirit? First you're going to have to make the decision to live by your spirit instead of being body-ruled. After you've made that decision, you can use the same principles of faith you use to believe for other needs in your life. In other words, you can apply the principles of faith to this area of taking control of your body, too, by *saying* what you believe according to God's Word (2 Cor. 4:13) and then *acting* upon what you have spoken (James 2:14, 17).

That's what Paul did. First, he had to *believe* that
according to God's Word, he was able to control his body
and bring it into subjection to his spirit (Phil. 4:13). Then
Paul *spoke* what he believed when he said, "I keep my
body under subjection" (1 Cor. 9:27). He made it a faith
statement. Then Paul *acted* on his faith as he daily pre-
sented his body as a living sacrifice to God and sowed to
his spirit instead of to his flesh (Rom. 12:1; Gal. 6:8).

Now let's look at what Jesus said about keeping the
body under subjection.

MATTHEW 18:8–9
**8   Wherefore if thy hand or thy foot offend thee, cut them
off, and cast them from thee: it is better for thee to enter
into life halt or maimed, rather than having two hands or
two feet to be cast into everlasting fire.
9   And if thine eye offend thee, pluck it out, and cast it
from thee: it is better for thee to enter into life with one
eye, rather than having two eyes to be cast into hell fire.**

Jesus wasn't talking about literally cutting off your hand
or foot or plucking out your eye. But He *was* saying you
must crucify any desire of your flesh that would cause you
to sin. You are to daily put to death the deeds of the flesh
(Rom. 8:13; Gal. 5:24). And sometimes when you make the
decision to stop doing something your flesh has enjoyed
doing for a long time, it will seem to hurt as much as it
would if you were to cut off your hand!

But if you want to walk closely with God and fulfill His
plan for your life, you must obey God's command to crucify the flesh, no matter how much your flesh dislikes it
(Gal. 5:24). Left to itself, your flesh will lead you into sin
and get you into trouble. You just have to accept the fact
that you have a body to contend with as long as you live
on this earth. Once you understand that, then determine

to crucify your flesh and keep your body under subjection to your spirit according to the Word.

One of the most important steps believers can take if they desire to listen to their hearts and live a spirit-ruled life is to *control what they say.* Actually, the Bible says the most difficult part of the body to keep under subjection is the tongue (James 3:8). This is not only true for the unsaved, but it is also true for believers.

For instance, some Christians who consider themselves moral, upright people still gossip about others. These believers wouldn't *think* of stealing, but if you want to know any rumors that are circulating within the Christian community, just go ask *them!* They will be glad to tell you all the gossip and slander they've heard. They hurt people with their words, yet they believe they are excelling in their Christian walk. They are deceiving themselves and dulling their ability to hear what the Holy Spirit is saying to their hearts.

Christians who refuse to crucify their flesh and stop gossiping should read the Book of James. James talks strongly about the consequences of *not* controlling the tongue.

JAMES 3:6
6 And the tongue is a fire, a world of iniquity: so is the tongue among our members, that it defileth the whole body, and setteth on fire the course of nature; and it is set on fire of hell.

Our words have the power to bring death or life into our lives (Prov. 18:21). If we would determine to control our tongues and speak only words that edify and bring life to people, we would save ourselves and others untold misery. Controlling the tongue is a vital part of keeping the body under subjection to the inward man. Unless you learn how to do this, it will hinder you from hearing from your spirit.

You might be thinking to yourself, *I haven't been doing a good job of keeping my body under in this area of controlling my tongue.* But if you are having trouble in this area, it's good to recognize that fact. The first step to conforming any area of your life to the Word of God is to admit you have a problem and that you've fallen short of God's Word. Then get yourself back in line with the Word.

The best way to get your tongue or any other part of your body under control is to find out what the Word says on that subject and be a doer of the Word whether you *feel* like it or not. Listen to what the Holy Spirit is prompting you to do and *make* your body obey His leading.

For instance, your body won't always want to get up and go to church on Sunday mornings. Your body would like you to lie in bed and think, *I worked too hard this week. I'll just lie here and listen to a tape.*

If you have been letting your tired body keep you from attending church regularly, your spirit needs to rise up and say, "Body, I don't care how hard you think you've worked—the Bible says we're not to forsake the assembling of ourselves together [Heb. 10:25]! You're going to church, whether you like it or not." It doesn't hurt to talk to your body that way if you need to. Just tell your body it's going to obey God's Word!

Your body should not dictate to you what you are going to do. *You* should dictate to your body what *it* is going to do. You need to be spirit-ruled like Smith Wigglesworth who used to say, "I don't *ask* Wigglesworth how he feels; I *tell* Wigglesworth how he feels!"

You are the only one who can bring your body under subjection to your spirit. If you don't, you will dull your sensitivity to what the Holy Spirit is saying to your heart. In fact, your entire Christian walk will be hindered if your body is not kept under subjection to your spirit.

Using the analogy of a runner in a race, the writer of Hebrews presents this same truth of keeping your body under subjection to your spirit so your Christian walk won't be hindered.

HEBREWS 12:1
1 Wherefore seeing we also are compassed about with so great a cloud of witnesses, let us LAY ASIDE EVERY WEIGHT, and the SIN which doth so easily beset us, and let us run with patience the race that is set before us.

We are to lay aside *anything* that might slow us down in the spiritual race God has set before us. I want you to notice this verse says to lay aside sins *and* weights. The word "weight" indicates there might be something in your life that is not necessarily sin, but if it hinders you from living totally committed to God, then it's a weight and should be laid aside. Otherwise, it's going to be harder for you to hear what the Holy Spirit speaks to your spirit.

When I ran track in high school, I learned how important it was to lay aside any weights that might slow me down in a race. Back then in the '50s, runners didn't have all the light equipment they do now. We practiced in heavy baseball shoes with metal cleats to build endurance. But when it came time to race, we switched to lighter-weight track shoes and took off everything we could that might weigh us down when we ran.

For instance, we would take off our watches and rings, and our track jerseys and shorts were made out of the lightest material possible. We even made our batons for the relay races out of balsa wood, the lightest wood available. We would get rid of every weight that might possibly slow us down because we wanted *to win the race*.

That's what you need to do in your *spiritual* race. If you want to fulfill God's plan for your life and win *your* race, you must examine your life in light of the Word of God. Sins or weights can keep you from hearing from the Holy Spirit and walking in the fullness of God's plan for you. Get quiet in your heart and ask the Holy Spirit to bring to your attention those things that need to be laid aside.

Make the decision to become spirit-ruled instead of body-ruled. Speak by faith, "I bring my body into subjection to my spirit." Then put action to your words by daily presenting your body to God and by laying aside any weights that hinder your spiritual growth so you can walk according to the Spirit. You can do it because the Bible says you can do *all* things through Christ who strengthens you (Phil. 4:13)!

That's how you run your race so you can win and achieve God's best in life (1 Cor. 9:24). And when you live your life with your body under the control of your spirit, you put yourself in a position to hear the Holy Spirit's leading. And if you will determine to always obey the Holy Spirit's direction, you will set yourself on a course to achieve success in every area of life!

Chapter 4
Training Your Human Spirit

This book of the law [God's Word] shall not depart out of thy mouth; but thou shalt MEDITATE therein day and night, that thou mayest OBSERVE TO DO according to all that is written therein: for then thou shalt make thy way prosperous, and THEN THOU SHALT HAVE GOOD SUCCESS.

—Joshua 1:8

If you want to be successful in every area of life, you must make the quality decision, "I'm going to listen to my heart and always do what the Holy Spirit is leading me to do." However, once you make that decision, don't expect to learn how to follow the leading of the Holy Spirit overnight. You must take steps to train and develop your spirit so you can be sensitive to the Holy Spirit's direction.

The training and developing of the human spirit is a new concept to many people. Most people understand the importance of training and developing their bodies, because there is a strong emphasis in this country on the need for physical fitness. Americans spend millions of dollars each year on the development of the physical body; and there's nothing wrong with a person endeavoring to get his body in shape. The Bible says "bodily exercise profits *little*" (1 Tim. 4:8). It doesn't say it doesn't profit at all!

Actually, a physically fit *body* can help ensure a fine-tuned *spirit*. For example, if a person is in poor physical condition and sluggish, it's probably going to be more difficult for him to be sensitive and in tune naturally or spiritually. On the other hand, being in good physical condition can make it easier for a person to be sensitive to spiritual things and yield to the Holy Spirit because discipline helps keep his body under subjection to his spirit (1 Cor. 9:27).

Besides the training of the physical body, millions of dollars are also spent each year at educational institutions on the developing of the intellect or the soulish part of man. And there is nothing wrong with developing our minds. In fact, it's good to continue to develop our intellects throughout our lives.

You should never stop learning about the world around you. Bookstores and libraries are full of good books, and most communities have educational programs where you can learn about a variety of subjects. Our world is changing quickly, and technology is advancing at a rapid pace. Unless you keep up with the changes by continuing to study and learn, it will be difficult to be successful in the natural realm.

Much time, energy, and money is expended yearly on the development of the physical and soulish parts of man. But what about the most important part of man—the spirit of man?

Even in the church world, little is taught about the need to develop the human spirit. Many Christians have the attitude that *God* is responsible for the development of their spirit. But the Bible tells us that God has already done everything He's going to do to redeem us through

Jesus Christ and to make us a success in every area of life—physically, mentally, *and* spiritually (Eph. 1:3; 2 Peter 1:3; 3 John 2).

2 PETER 1:3
3 According as his divine power HATH GIVEN unto us ALL THINGS that pertain unto life and godliness, through the knowledge of him that hath called us to glory and virtue.

You see, even though your spirit is made a new creature in Christ when you are born again (2 Cor. 5:17), your spirit still needs to be trained and developed. You don't grow from a baby Christian to a spiritually mature Christian overnight.

Of course, many people would like spiritual growth to occur that fast because it would be easier. For example, in the natural, the changes that result in growing up— growing pains—are not always comfortable. It's the same way spiritually.

For instance, do you remember your teenage years when you experienced certain physiological and emotional changes? In the natural, the transition from childhood to adulthood is sometimes uncomfortable. In a similar sense, you can go through certain uncomfortable stages in your spiritual growth too.

At different times in your life, you might grow spiritually to a certain plateau and then seem to stop progressing. At that point, the Holy Spirit might prompt you to make changes in areas of your life that do not line up with the Word. It might not always be easy, but in order to grow up spiritually and train your human spirit, walking in line with God's Word in every area of life is vitally important.

Just as your body and intellect must be trained and developed in order to use them to their fullest potential, so you must train and develop your *spirit* so it can reach its fullest potential. If you don't train your spirit, but instead allow your mind and your physical senses to dominate you, it will be difficult for you to accurately hear what the Holy Spirit is saying to you. God will not communicate with you through your mind or body. He is a Spirit (John 4:24), and He communicates with you through your *spirit*.

The Bible says clearly that *we* are responsible for our own spiritual growth (Rom. 12:1–2; Eph. 4:22–24; 1 Peter 2:2). If *we* don't train our spirits to be sensitive to the Holy Spirit's direction, it will never be done.

As a Christian, there are four important principles to follow in the training of your spirit (for further study on this subject, *see* also *How You Can Be Led by the Spirit of God* by Kenneth E. Hagin).

1. Meditate on the Word of God.

2. Practice the Word.

3. Give the Word first place in your life.

4. Instantly obey the voice of your spirit.

Let's look at the first principle in training your spirit: *Meditate on the Word of God.* The word "meditate" means *to focus one's thoughts on, to reflect on,* or *to ponder over.* You meditate on the Word of God by continually thinking on scriptures in your mind.

A person will never train his spirit if he only reads a psalm or a proverb a few minutes every morning. Some Christians take five minutes in the morning to pray a little prayer and read a small portion of Scripture. Then they say, "I've done my daily study of the Word, praise the Lord," and don't give the Scriptures another thought all day. Invariably, those Christians are weak spiritually because they haven't taken time to meditate on the Word to develop their spirits.

Don't just superficially read the Word of God. Instead, meditate on the scriptures the Lord has quickened to your heart. Whenever you have an opportunity during the day, roll scriptures over in your mind. Let God give you more light on those scriptures and expound on their meaning until the Word becomes a living reality in your spirit which the devil can never steal (Mark 4:15–20)!

I've made it my practice to meditate on the Word of God since I was young. For instance, when I was going to college, I worked the midnight shift at a plastic factory in Dallas, Texas. My responsibilities didn't take a lot of mental concentration, so I would meditate on scriptures while I worked.

I would read scriptures at home just before I left for work. Then all night long as I worked, I would reflect on those scriptures. I would meditate on the Word until it had gone from my mind down into my heart.

Reading scriptures in the morning and then meditating on them throughout the day is a good way to plant the Word deep in your heart and make it a part of your life (Ps. 119:11). Once a scripture has become a part of your heart, it is a continual nourishment to you and helps you train your spirit.

For instance, after hiding God's Word in your heart, you may not think about it again for a while. But if a crisis arises in your life pertaining to that particular scripture, when you get quiet inside and listen to your heart, that scripture will come up out of your spirit. And as you meditate on that scripture and confess it with your mouth, it will minister direction or comfort to you in the midst of the crisis.

God's words to Joshua before the Israelites entered the Promised Land tell us what happens in our lives when we *meditate on* and *obey* the Word of God: "*. . . then thou shalt make thy way PROSPEROUS, and then thou shalt have GOOD SUCCESS*" (Joshua 1:8).

It's obvious from this scripture that God wants us to be prosperous and have good success. Otherwise, He wouldn't have told Joshua how to prosper and succeed! Third John 2 says the same thing: "*Beloved, I wish above all things that thou mayest prosper and be in health, even as thy soul prospereth.*" God wants us to be a success in *every* area of our lives as we endeavor to develop our spirits.

However, notice it is not just a matter of meditating on the Word. God told Joshua to meditate on the Word so he could observe *to do* all that was written in the Word. That brings us to the second principle in training the human spirit: *Practice the Word.* As you become a doer of the Word you have been meditating upon, you will prosper and have good success in life.

There are many talkers *about* the Word, but not many doers *of* the Word. For instance, in my years of experience holding crusade meetings, I've seen people who really looked like they had the victory. When the congregation was praising God, they would jump higher and shout louder than anyone else.

But more than once I've had the opportunity to talk to some of these same people later on when they were facing a test or trial in their lives. When confronted with difficult circumstances, many of these people wouldn't be jumping, shouting, *or* praising God. Instead, they would cry, "What am I going to do now?"

I would tell them, "Do the same thing you were doing at the crusade meetings when things were going smoothly in your life. Shout praises to God because God never changes; the promises in His Word are still true!"

A doer of the Word praises God when circumstances in his life look bad, as well as when they look good, because his faith is not based on *what he sees*, but on *what God has said*.

If you have trained your spirit by practicing the Word, you won't be fretful because the Bible says, "Do not fret or have any anxiety about *anything* . . ." (Phil. 4:6 *Amp.*). Once you pray and ask God to meet your need, if you are a doer of the Word you won't wonder whether or not your prayer is going to be answered. Your heart is assured because you *know* you have your answer from God. Your answer may not have manifested yet, but your heart is full of joy and hope, not sadness and despair. If you are a doer of the Word, you rest in your faith in God's Word that your needs are met.

When you live each day practicing the Word you've put in your heart, you can go through any trial victoriously. The devil may try to make you think you are going under and that you're going to fail. But if you will refuse to be fretful or anxious and stand in faith on the promises of God's Word, then God's peace will guard your heart and mind in Christ Jesus (Phil. 4:6-7). Your heart will be at ease in the midst of the storms of life.

I learned a lot about how to be a doer of the Word from my father, Kenneth E. Hagin. As long as I can remember, he has walked in the peace of God, no matter what circumstances he faced.

For instance, I remember when I was about six years old, our family drove one hundred and fifty miles one night on an empty gas tank. We were on our way to my grandma's house in McKinney, Texas. We all called her Pat's Momma (Pat was the name of my dad's youngest brother).

Dad only had one dollar, so before we left that night for my grandmother's house, Dad stopped and put a dollar's worth of gas in the car. Then he got back in the car and prayed, "All right, Lord, I've been out on the field preaching for You, and now I have to get to McKinney. That one dollar was all the money I had. If I had more money, I would put more gas in the car. But I don't, so I expect this car to run. I expect You to take care of us just like You took care of the children of Israel."

Then Dad started the car and we drove out of that gas station without a care. We drove all the way to my grandma's house with no problem. However, once Dad turned the car off, we found out how empty the gas tank really was. When one of the family members closely inspected the gas tank, he couldn't even smell any fumes at all!

The gas gauge had registered empty for one hundred and fifty miles. In the natural, we couldn't have made it to McKinney. But the Word says our Heavenly Father takes care of His children (Matt. 7:9–11), and over the years Dad had trained his spirit with the Word so he could walk in God's supernatural provision.

I stayed up with Dad all through the night as we drove to visit Pat's Momma, and I watched him. My dad never once fretted about whether or not we would make it. He knew he had done his part in obeying God, and that God had promised to provide all of our needs (Phil. 4:19). Dad was operating in the *peace of God* because he had trained his spirit by being a doer of the *Word of God*. That made a big impression upon me as a little boy.

Another key to practicing the Word in your life is to practice the law of the New Testament—the law of love (John 13:34–35). Walking in love is an essential part of training your spirit and receiving direction for your life from the Holy Spirit.

When you understand that love is the fulfilling of the Law (Rom. 13:10), you won't be constantly concerned about whether or not you are fulfilling the Ten Commandments. In other words, when you walk in the love of God, you automatically fulfill the Ten Commandments.

When you walk in love, you won't lie about your neighbor; you won't steal from him. If you are walking in divine love, instead of coveting your neighbor's possessions, you will praise the Lord that he's been blessed!

Also, forgiving others is such an important part of walking in love. Never hold a grudge against anyone. That is one rule I live by in my own life. I never allow negative words someone has said to me or about me to lodge in my heart; I never allow my mind to dwell on such words. If I did, that would hinder my own fellowship with God, and I am not going to allow that.

If someone says or does something against me, I pray for him and leave the matter with God. But I refuse to hold a grudge. I'm determined to walk in love!

So let's practice the Word and practice walking in love. If you are not walking in love, you not only hinder your ability to listen to your heart, you hinder your ability to act on your faith in God's Word because love is the divine energy that causes faith to work (Gal. 5:6).

As you meditate on and practice the Word of God on a daily basis, you are *giving the Word first place in your life.* This is the third principle in training your spirit.

Jesus said, *". . . the words that I speak unto you, they are SPIRIT, and they are LIFE"* (John 6:63). You can feed on the Word of God until your heart and mind are saturated with the life of God. Then when you face a test or trial, you won't wonder what to do; you'll *know* what to do. The Word will reign so supreme in your life that no matter what you face, the first thing that comes out of your mouth is what *God's Word* says about the situation.

Early in life, my dad trained his spirit by feeding continually on the Word of God. And over the years I saw my father put the Word first in every situation and circumstance. For example, I remember standing with the family around the bed when my dad's mother, Pat's Momma, drew her last breath and went home to glory.

If you know anything about my dad's life and ministry, you've probably heard his story. His father left him when he was six years old and his mother sacrificed her own health as she tried to raise four children. Later when Dad was a sixteen-year-old boy, as he lay in bed sick and almost completely paralyzed for sixteen months, his mother took care of him.

So my dad was close to his mother and grateful for her loving care for him during those sixteen months when he was bedfast. And later in life, Dad tried to give his mother every comfort he possibly could. You can understand that in the natural her death would be painful to Dad.

But as the entire family stood around my grandmother's bed, I looked over at Dad and saw his lips moving. When you've lived with Dad as long as I have, you know that when he's talking quietly to himself, he's talking to God. So I began to listen to what he was saying, and I heard him quoting scriptures: *"O death, where is thy sting? O grave, where is thy victory?"* (1 Cor. 15:55). Scripture after scripture just began to roll out of his mouth.

At first Dad spoke quietly, but then he began to give voice to what the Holy Spirit was saying through him. And the Holy Spirit began to minister comfort to the entire family as scriptures about the death of God's saints poured out of Dad's spirit. For about ten minutes, Dad spoke scripture after scripture about the hope we have as saints and about our inheritance in Christ. And as Dad spoke the Word, the sadness and gloom that had pervaded the room disappeared and the comfort and peace of the Holy Ghost settled upon everyone.

Because Dad put the Word first in his life and trained his spirit with the Word, the Word sustained him in this crisis. If you'll meditate on the Word and practice it, it will be the same way with you. When you face a crisis in life, or when your body is hurting or you're hurting emotionally, the Word will be a sustaining comfort to you in your heart and mind. If you've been diligent to train your spirit with God's Word, the Word of God will be a soothing ointment that brings health and life into any situation you may face.

When you've saturated your mind and heart with the Word of God and have put it first in your life, it becomes much easier to practice the fourth principle in training your spirit man: *Instantly obey the voice of your spirit.* Remember, God through the Holy Spirit communicates with you through your recreated spirit, not through your head (Rom. 8:14, 16; 2 Cor. 5:17). So you learn to obey the

Holy Spirit's leading in your life as you learn to obey the voice of your own spirit.

I operate in my ministry and in my personal life according to this principle of instantly obeying my spirit. When I know in my spirit I need to make a decision based on the Word of God that doesn't necessarily make sense to the natural mind, I always obey what the Holy Spirit speaks to my heart.

You need to operate the same way in your life. When you *know* the Holy Spirit has spoken to your heart, instantly obey what God has told you to do. By doing this, you will grow up spiritually and bear much fruit in the Kingdom of God.

A businessman I know had an experience that is an excellent illustration of how important it is to instantly obey the voice of one's spirit. One day he was driving on an interstate highway on his way to a business appointment in a city two hundred miles away. He was going to that city to sign a $250,000 contract. He had timed his journey so he would arrive at his destination exactly on time for his appointment.

As this businessman drove down the highway to keep his appointment, he approached a road sign indicating the exit to a small town two miles off the highway. The Spirit of God spoke to his spirit and said, "Take that exit and go into that town." This businessman knew the voice of the Holy Spirit and was in the habit of instantly obeying the Holy Spirit's direction. So he prepared to take that exit, even though his appointment was in another city further down the road.

After taking the exit, the businessman stopped at a crossroads. The Holy Spirit said to him, "Turn right," so the man turned right. As he entered the small town, the

Holy Spirit told him, "Pull in over there." So the man pulled into a nearby parking lot, stopped his car and said, "All right, Lord. What now?"

The businessman didn't hear any further instructions from the Lord, so he just sat in his car and began to pray in other tongues. Remember, this man had an appointment to keep that would make him a lot of money, and time was slipping away! But he didn't get agitated. He stayed sensitive to the Holy Spirit and kept on praying.

Pretty soon a drunk fellow came stumbling down the street toward the businessman's car. The Holy Spirit again spoke to the businessman and said, "That man is why I sent you here. Go help him."

The businessman got out of his car and began ministering to the drunk man. As he talked to the man, he found out the man had lost everything that was precious to him because of his addiction to alcohol. Earlier that day, while lying in the city park, the man had looked up to Heaven and prayed, "If there is a God, please send someone to help me."

The businessman led the man to the Lord and then bought him a bus ticket so he could return to his family and make a new beginning for himself, living for the Lord. (When the businessman contacted the man some time later, he was still going strong in his walk with God!)

After ministering to the man, the businessman got back into his car and started down the highway, knowing he had missed his business appointment. But he just prayed, "Lord, I'll just let You take care of my business. It's *Your* business, anyway, not mine."

When he reached his destination, the secretary told him, "We've been trying to reach you. My boss was called out of town on an emergency and we had to reschedule your appointment for ten o'clock tomorrow morning." The next morning when the businessman arrived for his appointment, the other man told him, "Because I made you wait until this morning to close the deal, I'm going to give you an additional $10,000!"

When that businessman first heard the Holy Spirit's instruction to take that exit, he could have responded, "All right, let me go take care of my business deal, and then I'll come back and go into that town." But if he had done that, he wouldn't have been in the right place at the right time. The Holy Spirit knew the drunk man needed help *right then*.

Because this businessman instantly obeyed the Holy Spirit's direction, he became the answer to a desperate man's prayer. He not only led another soul into the Kingdom of God, he also closed his $250,000 business deal and received $10,000 as an added bonus! It pays to instantly obey the Holy Spirit.

Be diligent to practice these four principles for training your human spirit: Daily *meditate* on and *practice* the Word of God. Give the Word *first place* in your life. And instantly *obey* the voice of your spirit when you know the Lord has spoken to you. If you consistently practice these principles, you will develop your spirit and grow spiritually. And it won't be long before you will know in your spirit what to do in every situation you encounter in life.

Chapter 5

Learning to Follow the Inward Witness

. . . for YE ARE THE TEMPLE OF THE LIVING GOD; as God hath said, I will dwell IN them, and walk IN them; and I will be their God, and they shall be my people.
—2 Corinthians 6:16

The Bible says that you as a believer are the temple of the living God (1 Cor. 3:16; 2 Cor. 6:16). If you are going to learn how to follow your heart in every situation, that remarkable truth must become a living reality in your daily life. You cannot learn to respond to situations from your heart unless you are ever conscious of the Presence of the Holy Spirit *dwelling within* your spirit to guide and direct you in every area of life.

The Holy Spirit communicates with you through your spirit where He dwells. So you don't need to go looking for God to speak a word to you through others. God may *confirm* through others what He has already said to you in your own spirit. But for the most part God isn't going to use prophets or spectacular supernatural events to guide you in the affairs of life. He's going to lead you by the Holy Spirit speaking to your spirit (Rom. 8:14, 16).

You can get so taken up seeking guidance through others that you miss what God is saying to your own heart. God wants you to train your human spirit so you can walk closely with Him. As you do that, you will get to the

41

place where you can hear Him clearly when He speaks to you through your spirit.

The number one way God leads us is through the *inward witness* of the Holy Spirit in our spirits. Some people describe it as an *"inward intuition."* That's just a different term referring to the same thing.

The inward witness of the Holy Spirit is an inner *knowing*, and it will never contradict the Word of God. With the inward witness, you don't always know how or why you know something, but what you know is as real on the inside of you in your spirit as if someone had spoken to your natural ear. That inner knowing is the Holy Spirit bearing witness with your own spirit to give you wisdom, guidance, comfort—whatever you need at a particular moment.

Any believer can be led by the inward witness of the Holy Spirit. In fact, sometimes a baby Christian can be more sensitive to the inward witness than some older Christians who have never developed their spirit.

Baby Christians are usually very aware of the dramatic change that took place on the inside of them when they became new creatures in Christ. Often new converts are so conscious of the Holy Spirit's indwelling Presence that it's easy for them to follow the direction of the Holy Spirit as He speaks to their heart.

For instance, sometimes when new converts hear wrong doctrine being taught, they instinctively know in their spirit something isn't right, even though they may not know much about the Bible yet. Over the years, I've had baby Christians tell about certain meetings, saying, "I just knew there was something wrong with what that preacher taught." These baby Christians hadn't been born again long enough to *intellectually* understand the doctrinal problems in the sermons they'd heard; they just picked it up in their *spirit*.

On the other hand, sometimes people who have been Christians for years aren't very sensitive to the inward witness. Many times they have an apathetic attitude and don't esteem the indwelling Presence of the Holy Spirit as they should. That keeps them from being attuned to the Holy Spirit's leading within their own heart.

For example, I've heard of supposedly "mature" Christians going to meetings where some minister was preaching wrong doctrine, and they swallowed it hook, line, and sinker! They didn't even bother to compare it with the Word or to check their spirit for the Holy Spirit's warning. Many times Christians accept what is said without checking it against the Bible just because the minister is well known or has a big ministry.

When some of these more "mature" Christians recognize they've missed it, many times they say, "You know, when I first heard that teaching, something about it bothered me, but I didn't know what it was. But because that minister was well known, I went along with it."

I don't care who is preaching, if you have a check in your spirit about what's being said, listen to what your spirit is trying to tell you! Study the Scriptures and see if the teaching lines up with the Word.

Always make the Word of God your standard for truth. If you make the Word your standard, it will help you train your spirit. For example, you don't need to check with the Holy Spirit indwelling your spirit to see if it's all right for you to marry an unbeliever. The Bible already plainly tells you it is *not* right (2 Cor. 6:14–18), and the Holy Spirit will never tell you anything different from the Word. Anytime the Holy Spirit speaks to your spirit, it will always be in line with the Word.

Becoming sensitive to the inward witness of the Holy Spirit is the responsibility of *every* Christian. God's design for His children is that they be led by His Holy Spirit in *every* area of life—spiritually, physically, emotionally, intellectually, socially, and financially (Rom. 8:14, 16).

We desperately need the Holy Spirit's guidance in order to deal wisely in all the affairs of life. In today's society we're continually confronted with so many decisions— from minor decisions such as which car to buy to major decisions about career and marriage. God wants to give us counsel and wisdom not only in these major decisions which affect the course of our lives, but also in the small matters of life.

So don't limit God in your life by only seeking His guidance for matters you think are "big" enough for God to be concerned about. God wants to guide and direct you in your personal life, in your job or ministry, in your leisure activities, and in your relationships with other people. God is interested in *everything* you do.

It's important to check your spirit and receive the Holy Spirit's counsel in making decisions or when you need wisdom to solve a problem. For instance, if a conflict arises between you and another person, begin to seek God about the matter. As you listen to your heart, the Holy Spirit will show you the source of the problem and give you wisdom to change the situation.

It's also important to listen to your heart because the Holy Spirit might want to use you to help someone in need. For example, recently a Rhema student was able to help save someone's life because he heard and obeyed the Holy Spirit's direction to his own spirit.

This Rhema student worked at an auto body shop near Rhema. Late one night he had a strong urging to close the shop an hour early and leave immediately. The Rhema student listened to his heart and obeyed the Holy Spirit's leading.

As the Rhema student stepped outside to lock the shop door, he heard a noise that sounded like someone groaning. The groaning stopped, and seeing nothing, he went to his car. Just as he reached his car, he heard the moaning again. Then he saw a small light on the ground across the street. He went to investigate and found a man lying unconscious on the grass next to a wrecked motorcycle.

The injured man had no identification on him except that he was wearing a cross pendant around his neck. The Rhema student laid hands on him and prayed that he would live and not die and then ran back to the shop to phone for help. While he was waiting for the ambulance to arrive, the Rhema student went back to the injured man and spoke the Word of God over him. Within a few minutes the ambulance arrived and rushed the man to the hospital.

Later this Rhema student found out that the injured man was a fellow Rhema student who had lost control of his motorcycle on the dark, winding street. Despite extensive injuries, the injured student experienced a miraculous recovery in just a short period of time. Doctors told him that most people in his condition don't *live*, much less fully recover!

Praise God for the inward witness of the Holy Spirit! In the late evening hours, the street where this motorcycle accident occurred is dark and usually deserted. Without the Holy Spirit's guidance, the injured Rhema student might not have received help until the next morning.

The Holy Spirit knew the injured young man needed help immediately, so He found a believer nearby who knew how to hear His Voice. The Holy Spirit guided that believer to the right place at the right time to help someone in need. How important it is to be led by the Holy Spirit, whether in small matters or in times of crisis!

A believer needs to know how to hear and obey the leading of the Holy Spirit if he is going to be successful in *any* area of life. For instance, my dad tells a story about a businessman in Texas who rose from poverty to great wealth because he learned how to follow the Holy Spirit's direction. This man earned his fortune by making investments, and over a period of many years, he never lost one penny on any investment! When asked about the key to his success, he said, "I learned to listen to what the Spirit of God speaks to my own spirit."

The businessman explained how he made decisions regarding investments. He said, "There have been business deals that on paper seemed sure to succeed. Yet the Holy Spirit on the inside of me said, 'Don't do it.' Then there have been other deals which on paper looked like certain failures. My natural mind said, 'This will never succeed.' But the Holy Spirit on the inside of me said, 'Invest in that deal.'"

The businessman said, "I have always listened to my spirit and obeyed the Holy Spirit's leading. If I'm not able to immediately get an answer on a particular deal, I spend time in the Word and in prayer until I *know* what the Holy Spirit is saying to my spirit."

Because that businessman had trained his spirit and had made it a practice to follow his spirit in business matters, he never lost money on any investment. He experienced success in life because he learned how to listen to his heart and be sensitive to the inward witness of the Holy Spirit.

A key ingredient to this businessman's success in hearing and obeying the Holy Spirit's leading was *quality time spent in the Word and in prayer.* A person cannot learn to listen to his heart without spending time fellowshipping with God through His Word and in prayer and by diligently seeking Him.

Let me give you some practical advice about waiting on God to receive guidance. If you spend time in prayer to receive God's wisdom about a specific situation, don't get frustrated if you don't immediately receive an answer. After you've asked God for wisdom, you should keep thanking Him that He answered you when you prayed (Mark 11:24; James 1:5–6). However, the guidance you need might come when you least expect it.

In my own life I've found that God often speaks to me some time *after* I have prayed about a particular situation. He usually speaks to me when I'm relaxed and my mind is quiet enough to hear the Holy Spirit in my heart. For instance, I might be shaving in the morning or relaxing as I watch a football game on television when I suddenly receive revelation from the Holy Spirit about something I prayed about days or even weeks before.

Often when we pray for wisdom about a specific situation, our minds are so cluttered with the details of our daily lives that we have a difficult time listening to what the Holy Spirit is saying to our hearts. That's why we often receive revelation from the Lord when our minds are quiet and our hearts are open.

Don't allow yourself to become frustrated as you wait on God for His guidance. Instead, continue to thank

Him in faith for giving you the wisdom you asked for. As you do that, the Holy Spirit will direct you in the small *and* the big affairs of life so you can lead a successful Christian life.

Let me give you another example of a person who became successful by following the Holy Spirit's direction in his heart. One of our board members started out in business for himself with about $5,500. In his spirit he sensed the Lord leading him to invest his money in a particular area. But he began listening to people who told him that to stay financially sound, he needed to diversify his investments. So he made business decisions based on other people's "sensible" advice and his own mental reasonings, and he lost all his money except for fifty dollars.

About that time this man got one of Brother Hagin's cassette tapes, "How to Train the Human Spirit," which presents scriptural principles for developing one's spirit. He began listening to this tape over and over again until the truth of God's Word was planted deep in his heart. Then he began acting upon those principles by training his spirit and learning how to follow his heart.

This board member began investing money in a particular area as God had originally instructed him to do. And as he obeyed the inward witness of the Holy Spirit, he became more and more successful in business. Today his business is worth millions of dollars. He learned that it pays to listen to his heart!

You need to learn that same lesson. You will encounter people throughout life who will try to give you advice and convince you that they know what they are talking about. But there will be times in life when you have to shut out all the other voices in the world and listen only to what God tells you.

For example, many times economic experts would advise you to either invest or save your money according to the present economic state of the nation. But the Bible says, *"Blessed is the man that walketh not in the counsel of the ungodly . . ."* (Ps. 1:1). That doesn't mean we are not to use the natural wisdom and knowledge God has given us. But, on the other hand, if God tells you to do something, and experts advise the opposite, you can only be blessed by following God's counsel rather than man's advice.

For instance, several years ago God began speaking to the leadership of this ministry about beginning a large building project. We met with our board members, all of whom are successful Spirit-filled businessmen. We said to them, "We realize the nation's economic indicators make undertaking this project at this time seem unwise in the natural. But we know we've heard from the Lord in this matter."

One of our board members, a very successful businessman, spoke up and said, "Brother Hagin, I believe we need to act on what God is leading you to do. The Word of God which you teach says to obey God and to ignore the counsel of the ungodly if it contradicts what God has instructed you to do [Ps. 1:1]. I've always put that principle into practice in my own business with great success."

The board member continued, "I pray about every business decision I make. If I get an inward witness or leading about a transaction, but economic experts advise me not to do it, I always obey God. That's why I'm where I am today financially. Now if God doesn't specifically give me direction, then I look at the economic indicators and act accordingly."

That's combining spiritual wisdom with practical wisdom—and the natural and the supernatural coming
together make an explosive force for God!

So with the board's approval, we obeyed God and began
the large building project, as God had instructed us. And
despite the poor economy at that time, everything worked
out well. The truth is, when this ministry has undertaken
anything God has told us to do, following the Lord's leading every step of the way, success has always been the
outcome!

Let me say this simply as a word of caution. If you
make a decision to go against natural wisdom and economic indicators to the contrary, you must be assured
beyond any shadow of doubt that God has told you to do
so. You can't just do something hoping that God is in it
and expect Him to provide the needed finances to bail you
out. I've seen many people, even ministers, do that and
when the project didn't succeed, they claimed that God
had failed them. No, God never fails. They were the ones
at fault because they didn't take the time to hear from
God correctly. If God tells you to do something and you
continually follow His leading as you do it, it will succeed.

Obeying the inward witness of the Holy Spirit is abso-
lutely essential to being a successful Christian. Don't try
to measure your success by comparing yourself with other
people. Just be diligent to obey the Holy Spirit's leading
in every situation of life and trust God to prosper whatever you put your hand to (Joshua 1:8; Ps. 1:1–3).

God does not measure your success in life by comparing
you with your peers or fellow church members. He accepts
you and works with you where you are in your Christian
walk. And He sees you as successful *if you are obeying*

Him and doing what He told you to do. That's why it's so important to learn how to obey the inward witness and follow the Holy Spirit's leading in your heart.

You *can* be the successful Christian God designed you to be. You *can* train your spirit to become sensitive to the inward witness of the Holy Spirit. In every situation you face in life, you can learn to respond from your *heart*, not from your head or from your physical senses. You are the temple of the Holy Spirit, and He will faithfully guide you in every area of life as you learn how to hear His Voice and follow His leading.

Chapter 6

Why Believers Sometimes Fail to Follow Their Hearts

For as many as are led by the Spirit of God, they are the sons of God.

—Romans 8:14

The Bible tells us that every child of God should be led by the Holy Spirit in every affair of life. Yet so many times believers fail to hear and heed the inward witness of the Holy Spirit. And sometimes there are unpleasant consequences to suffer when believers don't listen to their heart—their recreated spirit.

I want to discuss some of the reasons believers fail to follow the Holy Spirit's leading in their heart. What causes some people to travel down a road to failure in life? Learning from our mistakes and the mistakes of others can help us avoid the same pitfalls. We can choose instead to take the road to success as we follow God's plan for our lives by listening to the Holy Spirit speak to our heart.

One reason many believers fail to follow their heart is they've never been taught how to train their human spirit. Instead, many believers have been trained all of their lives to listen to what their intellect or their five physical senses tell them. They were taught early in life to lean to their own understanding or human reasoning (Prov. 3:5), rather than to get quiet on the inside in their spirit and listen to what the Holy Spirit is telling them.

Believers sometimes continue to experience failure in their lives because they've kept their spirit locked up or undeveloped inside of them, so God is hindered from communicating with them like He wants to.

God wants to lead believers in every area of life. For instance, the Holy Spirit may try to warn a person of impending danger through the inward witness. However, if that person spends all of his time only feeding his intellect, not his spirit, he may not recognize the warnings of the Holy Spirit. Thinking it is just a passing thought in his own head, he might ignore the Holy Spirit's warning and then suffer the consequences. But a person who takes time to feed his spirit through meditating on the Word and through prayer is better prepared to hear the Holy Spirit and to instantly obey His leading.

Also, believers who continually keep their spirit locked up and undeveloped and have never learned to listen to their heart become easy prey to every wind of doctrine that sweeps through the Church. These believers are often taken advantage of by "spiritual con artists" who are out looking for someone to deceive.

For instance, over the years we've had some students who came to attend Rhema with ample money to pay their tuition, but they fell prey to spiritual con artists who told them a sad story of their desperate need. Out of compassion and ignorance, some of these Rhema students gave these spiritual cons their own tuition money because they thought they were being led of the Lord to do so; then they had no money to pay their own tuition.

After a few weeks of taking money from naive students, these con artists dropped out of Rhema with cash in hand. If these students had recognized the witness of the Holy Spirit on the inside, they never would have fallen prey to these con artists in the first place.

I've heard my dad tell a story that is a good example of a believer who was actually swindled because she didn't listen to her spirit. This woman was in the ministry; she was a pastor. A big-name evangelist came to hold citywide meetings in the town where she pastored, and her church helped sponsor this evangelist's meetings.

Before the meetings began, the evangelist convinced this woman pastor to pay the $3,000 rental fee for the building where the meetings would be held. The evangelist assured the woman that he would pay her back from the offerings collected at the meetings.

The meetings were successful and the evangelist received good offerings every night. However, when the meetings were over, the evangelist left town with all the offering money, leaving this woman pastor to pay not only the building rental fee, but the entire budget for the meetings, totaling $5,000!

But this woman pastor wasn't the kind of person to accept being cheated. She found out where this evangelist was holding his next meeting and went to that city to confront him. While the meeting was in progress, this pastor walked up the aisle onto the platform and sat down beside the evangelist.

The woman pastor told the evangelist, "I've got my briefcase with me. Each night when it's time to receive an offering, I'm going to come up on the platform and take the offering myself. And I'm going to keep on doing that every night until I get my five thousand dollars."

The evangelist exclaimed, "No, you can't do that!"

The woman pastor said, "If you don't let me do that, I'm going to get up on this platform and tell the audience how you cheated me when you held meetings in my city." Needless to say, that pastor got her money back!

When this woman pastor later talked to my dad and mom about the incident, she told them, "When that evangelist came to me and asked me to pay the building rental fee, something inside me kept saying, 'Don't do it.' But my head kept telling me, 'Well, he's a good evangelist. And his meetings are needed in this town.' So I listened to my head and paid the money."

The woman pastor concluded, "I could have saved myself a plane ticket and a lot of trouble if I had only listened to my spirit!" That's true for every one of us. We'd all save ourselves a lot of trouble if we would learn how to listen to the Holy Spirit's direction in our spirit!

So one reason believers fail to follow their heart is they haven't been taught how to train their human spirit and become sensitive to the Holy Spirit's inward leading. Another reason believers fail to follow their heart is similar to the first reason: Many believers become too busy with natural affairs to get quiet inside and listen to what the Holy Spirit is saying to their spirit.

For instance, I remember Dad talking about one of his pastor friends who had three serious automobile accidents in less than ten years. People were killed, and he himself was seriously injured. In one of the accidents, his wife escaped death only by God's miraculous intervention.

After this pastor and his wife had fully recovered from their injuries, Dad preached in their church on how to be led by the Holy Spirit. After the pastor heard Dad's teaching on the subject, he told Dad, "If I had understood ten years ago about being led by the Holy Spirit, I never would have had those three car accidents."

Then the pastor made a significant statement to Dad: "Before every one of those accidents, I had a feeling that something wasn't right. But each time I thought, *We're in a hurry to get to our destination because I have so much to do!* I was too busy to stop long enough to pray and find out what the Lord was trying to say to me."

In today's high-pressure society, it's easy to become too busy to get quiet inside and listen for the Holy Spirit's leading. But we need to take listening to our heart seriously. We need to pay attention if we get an uneasiness or a "check" in our spirit about a person or a situation. The Holy Spirit wants to guide us in our lives and help us avoid the devil's snares and pitfalls.

An important part of avoiding the devil's snares is to daily claim God's protection over your family. I personally do that in my devotions every morning. Appropriating God's protection by *faith*—not out of *fear*—is one of your covenant rights in Christ Jesus (Ps. 91:1–16; Heb. 8:6).

However, one way God protects you is to show you things to come that you need to know (John 16:13). So as you pray and claim God's protection, it is also important to listen to your heart as you go about your daily tasks. Stay sensitive to the Holy Spirit's voice.

For instance, since the Holy Spirit knows the future, He might prompt you to delay your departure for work one morning or to take a different route than usual in order to prevent an automobile accident. But if you haven't trained your spirit to be sensitive to the Holy Spirit's leading, you might not recognize that prompting as the inward witness of the Spirit.

It's possible to live your life continually overriding your spirit. In other words, it's possible to become so busy with the natural activities in life that when the Holy Spirit tries to get your attention, you don't hear what your heart is trying to tell you. Instead you act on what your head and your physical senses tell you.

If you ignore the Holy Spirit's promptings, eventually those promptings will grow weaker and weaker. The Holy Spirit is a gentleman; He won't intrude where He is not wanted. He won't force you to listen and obey His direction. The Holy Spirit only guides and directs those who open the door to Him and invite Him to lead and guide them. In other words, the Holy Spirit guides those who take the time to listen to their heart and obey His leading.

That brings us to another reason believers sometimes fail to follow their heart: They follow plans of their own making instead of the Holy Spirit's leading. In other words, sometimes when believers need to make a decision and the Holy Spirit is trying to give them direction, they don't want to listen to what He's saying to them. They want to pursue their own desires. Their head tells them it would be more advantageous to do things their own way, so they shut off the voice of their spirit and listen to their own mental reasoning. That's when they get into trouble.

For instance, I've seen some people who had a call to the full-time ministry quit their job prematurely because they thought it was time for them to begin their own ministry. They wanted to fulfill the call of God on their life so much that they left their job before it was God's time and pursued a plan of their own making. They weren't ready yet to go out on their own, but they didn't take time to wait before God in prayer to get the Holy Spirit's leading. And because they weren't adequately prepared and were pursuing their own plan, they made a mess of things and had to backtrack to where they missed it.

Many of these people recognized where they missed God and later admitted, "If I'd listened to my spirit, I wouldn't have stepped out so quickly. But I wanted to start my own ministry, and I thought leaving my job was the way to succeed." No, the way to succeed is to do *what* God tells you to do *when* God tells you to do it.

It's so important to wait for God's timing before you act on the direction you've received from the Lord. Failing to move in God's timing is the same as moving out of His will. So when you know God has given you specific guidance, that's not the time to stop listening for the Holy Spirit's direction. Continue to pray and wait on God. The Spirit of God on the inside of you will tell you when it's the *right time* to do what He's told you to do.

Let me give you an illustration from my own experience about waiting on God's timing. In 1972, Mama and Papa Goodwin, two highly respected ministers whom my family had known for years, spoke a word from the Lord to me through tongues and interpretation (1 Cor. 12:10). They said God would give me a special anointing to minister to the sick. It was a word from the Lord, but I didn't step out and try to make it happen. In fact, it was *five years* later when I actually began to operate in that anointing.

For five years I waited on God's timing for the healing anointing to operate in my life. Then in 1977, in the prayer room before a crusade meeting in Texas, the Spirit of God moved on one of our singers. This singer spoke out the same thing that the Holy Spirit had already spoken to my own heart.

The Holy Spirit said that it was time to step out and begin to minister to the sick with the special healing anointing God had given me. I obeyed God and ministered to the sick with a new anointing that night. And from that night to the present time, I have continued to minister to the sick with that strong healing anointing.

You see, once you hear from God, you need to let things happen *the way* God wants them to happen, *when* He wants them to happen. Don't try to make God's counsel to you come to pass in your own strength. When you get ahead of God, you make problems for yourself, and you hinder God from accomplishing His plan for you. God's plan and purpose for your life will only be fulfilled as you *follow* God instead of trying to run ahead of Him and make things happen in your own strength and timing.

Some people have told us that we've taken too much time in building the many buildings on the Rhema campus. But, actually, we have been right on schedule. And because we've followed God's plan and timing, we don't have a huge debt to pay off. We could have built Rhema much more quickly, but we would have been out of step with God.

Someone might say, "But I thought God told you to build Rhema." Yes, God did tell us to build Rhema. But even though God tells us to do something, we still have to listen to our spirit in order to find out *how* and *when* He wants us to do it!

You need to train your human spirit to stay *in step* with God's will and His timing in every situation of life. Don't get ahead of God's timing. On the other hand, don't hold back when the Holy Spirit prompts you to take the next step in God's plan for you either.

I said that instantly obeying the voice of your spirit is the fourth principle to follow in training your spirit. You stay in step with God as you instantly obey the voice of your spirit, whether the Holy Spirit tells you to take a step of faith or to wait on Him for His timing and direction. You see, instantly obeying your spirit does *not* mean you always immediately move on every leading of the Holy Spirit. It can also mean you immediately begin to seek God for further direction about His plan.

For instance, if the Holy Spirit gives you direction for your future, but you aren't sure of God's timing, you need to wait before God until you know exactly when to act on what He's told you to do. Waiting on God for His timing is still obeying your spirit. On the other hand, if the Holy Spirit tells you to immediately act on what He has told you to do, then the time to obey is *right then*, not the next day!

Sometimes when the Holy Spirit prompts believers to take a step of obedience, they're hindered from immediately obeying what God is telling them to do because *they won't let go of the past*. That's another reason believers can fail to follow their heart.

God had something to say to the prophet Samuel about letting go of the past. Samuel had grieved over God's rejection of Saul as Israel's king.

1 SAMUEL 15:35
35 And Samuel came no more to see Saul until the day of his death: nevertheless SAMUEL MOURNED FOR SAUL: and the Lord repented that he had made Saul king over Israel.

1 SAMUEL 16:1
1 And the Lord said unto Samuel, HOW LONG WILT THOU MOURN for Saul, seeing I have rejected him from reigning over Israel? FILL THINE HORN WITH OIL, and GO, I will send thee to Jesse the Bethlehemite: for I have provided me a king among his sons.

In essence, God told Samuel, "Don't mourn any longer over Saul because I have rejected him as Israel's king." You see, Saul's heart was not right before God. Saul had rebelled against God's commands and had lost his kingdom because of his disobedience.

But Samuel continued to mourn over Saul's failure. God wanted Samuel to stop mourning over the past so he could take the *next* step in God's plan for Israel and anoint someone else as the new king.

Some believers do the same thing Samuel did: They hinder themselves from taking the next step in God's plan for their lives because they continue to mourn over their past failures and mistakes. They continually accuse themselves, thinking, *I didn't go when God told me to go,* or *I jumped out ahead of God and made a mess of everything.* And condemnation about past failures keeps them from obeying God when He speaks to them.

Believers who are grieving over past failures need to do what God told Samuel to do. After He told Samuel to stop mourning over the past, God instructed Samuel to ". . . *FILL THINE HORN WITH OIL, and GO . . .*" (1 Sam. 16:1). In other words, believers who are mourning over the past need to get before God, receive God's forgiveness for past failures, and let go of the past once and for all.

Then they need to allow God to fill them anew with a fresh anointing of the Holy Spirit. Once their "horn is filled with oil," they will be ready to "go." I don't necessarily mean they will move from their physical surroundings, but they will be able to go on with God and be better able to listen to their heart and obey the Holy Spirit's leading in their life.

Another reason believers sometimes fail to follow their heart is that they want to understand the whole picture of God's plan for them before they will take even one step of obedience. But God doesn't lead us that way. He leads us one step at a time.

For instance, when the prophet Samuel obeyed God and traveled to Jesse's house to anoint the new king, he didn't know which of Jesse's sons was God's choice for Israel. Samuel took a step of obedience by doing what he knew to do—he went to Jesse's house. He did what he knew to do and then expected God to lead him further once he arrived at Jesse's house.

God didn't immediately tell Samuel who His choice was for king. Samuel had to walk by faith and obedience. God allowed Samuel to meet each of the young men, and seven times He told Samuel, "No, that's *not* My choice" (1 Sam. 16:4–10). Finally, when David stood before Samuel, God said to Samuel, "He's the one" (1 Sam. 16:12)! That was the revelation Samuel needed in order to obey God's instruction to anoint the next king of Israel.

The Holy Spirit often leads us the same way—one step at a time. If we sense the Holy Spirit's leading to take a step of obedience, we should take that step based on what God has told us to do. We don't have to know God's whole plan for us in order to take the first step of obedience. God promises to direct our paths as we obey Him to the best of our knowledge and stay sensitive to the Holy Spirit's leading (Prov. 3:5–6). If we make a wrong move, the Holy Spirit will speak to our heart, "No, don't go that way. Go this way instead" (Isa. 30:21).

For instance, sometimes I have an inward witness that some situation in our ministry offices needs my attention, but many times that's all I know. With more than twenty departments and more than two hundred employees, I need the Holy Spirit's leading in order to know what to do. So I begin walking through every building on the campus. I go into every department, staying sensitive to my heart.

Usually I know on the inside when I reach the department that needs my attention. Once I know *where* to concentrate my attention, the next step is to discover *what* the situation is that needs my attention. In cases like this, the Holy Spirit leads me step by step. Whatever the situation is, He gives me wisdom and counsel to know how to deal with it.

As you learn how to follow your heart, you must accept the fact that God is going to lead you one step at a time. God won't give you the whole picture all at once, although at times, He will show you things to come (John 16:13). Most of the time God gives you just one step of His plan for you and then expects you to walk by faith and stay sensitive to your spirit so you can hear Him when He is ready to give you the next step.

God's Word is a *lamp* to our feet and a *light* to our path (Ps. 119:105), but that doesn't mean a giant floodlight lights up our path for miles ahead! In other words, God doesn't give us detailed instructions revealing His plan for the next ten years!

That isn't what this verse is saying. Using modern terms, God's leading in our lives through His Word is more like a *flashlight* on our path. He shines His light on our path so we can take one or two steps. As we take those steps, the "flashlight" of His Word and His Spirit light up the next step we are to take.

However, if we never move, His light won't light up those next steps. In other words, there are times in our lives when we must take the *first* step of obedience before God will reveal the *next* step He wants us to take.

We've looked at several reasons why people sometimes fail to follow their heart. You should allow those reasons to become "signposts" for you which point you *away* from danger *toward* the road to successfully following God.

Learn to follow the Holy Spirit's leading one step at a time. Keep in step with God as He unfolds His plan for you. Don't jump out too quickly in His plan, nor lag behind the Holy Spirit's leading. Don't allow your past to keep you from obeying God in the present, and guard your heart from being sidetracked by your own ambitions and desires. Above all, never get so busy with natural affairs that you lose touch with your heart and miss what the Holy Spirit is saying to you.

There are many things you as a believer need to learn in life, but nothing is more important than learning how to listen to the Holy Spirit's direction to your heart. You have the Spirit of the Almighty God living inside your recreated spirit to guide and direct you. Make sure you always esteem His indwelling Presence by staying sensitive to His leading.

The Holy Spirit's Presence within you is a continuous miracle and a precious Gift, given by a loving Heavenly Father who wants you to be successful in every area of your life. So develop your spirit by the Word of God and always allow the Holy Spirit to lead you. Receiving the counsel and wisdom you need for every situation you encounter in life is easy as you learn to listen to your heart!

Why should you consider attending

Rhema
Bible Training College?

Here are a few good reasons:

- Training at one of the top Spirit-filled Bible schools anywhere
- Teaching based on steadfast faith in God's Word
- Growth in your spiritual walk coupled with practical training in effective ministry
- Specialization in the area of your choosing: Youth or Children's Ministry, Evangelism, Pastoral Care, Missions, Biblical Studies, or Supportive Ministry
- Optional intensive third- and fourth-year programs: School of Worship, School of Pastoral Ministry, School of World Missions, School of Biblical Studies, and General Extended Studies
- Worldwide ministry opportunities—while you're in school
- An established network of churches and ministries around the world who depend on Rhema to supply full-time staff and support ministers
- A two-year evening school taught entirely in Spanish is also available. Log on to **www.cebrhema.org** for more information.

**Call today or go online for more
information or application material.**

1-888-28-FAITH (1-888-283-2484)

www.rbtc.org

Rhema Bible Training College admits students of any race, color, or ethnic origin.

OFFER CODE—BKORD:PRMDRBTC

Rhema Word Partner Club

WORKING *together* TO REACH THE WORLD!

People. Power. Purpose.

Have you ever dropped a stone into water? Small waves rise up at the point of impact and travel in all directions. It's called a ripple effect. That's the kind of impact Christians are meant to have in this world—the kind of impact that the Rhema family is producing in the earth today.

The Rhema Word Partner Club links Christians with a shared interest in reaching people with the Gospel and the message of faith in God.

Together we are reaching across generations, cultures, and nations to spread the Good News of Jesus Christ to every corner of the earth.

To join us in reaching the world,
visit **www.rhema.org/wpc** or call **1-866-312-0972**.

Always on.

For the latest news and information on products, media, podcasts, study resources, and special offers, visit us online 24 hours a day.

Word of Faith

Free Subscription!

Call now to receive a free subscription to *The Word of Faith* magazine from Kenneth Hagin Ministries. Receive encouragement and spiritual refreshment from . . .

- *Faith-building articles from Kenneth W. Hagin, Lynette Hagin, Craig W. Hagin, and others*

- *"Timeless Teaching" from the archives of Kenneth E. Hagin*

- *Feature articles on prayer and healing*

- *Testimonies of salvation, healing, and deliverance*

- *Children's activity page*

- *Updates on Rhema Bible Training College, Rhema Bible Church, and other outreaches of Kenneth Hagin Ministries*

Subscribe today for your free *Word of Faith*!

1-888-28-FAITH (1-888-283-2484)

www.rhema.org/wof

OFFER CODE—BKORD:WF